New Year's SEO Resolutions for Your Business

Terry Power

Table of Contents

Introduction

- **Purpose**: Inspire small business owners to use the New Year as a starting point for elevating their SEO and digital marketing strategies.
- **Tone**: Practical yet motivational, showing that small changes can yield big results.

Chapter 1: New Year, New Opportunities: Why SEO Matters for Small Businesses

- Overview of SEO's importance in 2024 and beyond.
- The power of local SEO in driving foot traffic and leads.
- Inspirational examples: Small businesses that achieved success through SEO.

Chapter 2: Setting Goals for SEO Success

- Identifying realistic and impactful goals for small business SEO.
- Practical framework: SMART (Specific, Measurable, Achievable, Relevant, Time-bound) goals for SEO.
- Checklist: How to audit your current SEO standing.

Chapter 3: Local SEO: Capturing Your Community's Attention

- Introduction to local SEO and its relevance for small businesses.
- Actionable tips: Optimizing Google Business Profile and local keywords.
- Example: A bakery using local SEO to dominate its city's search results.

Chapter 4: The Power of Keywords: Speaking Your Customers' Language

- Why keywords are essential and how to research them effectively.
- Tools for keyword research (free and paid).
- Checklist: How to organize and implement keyword research findings.

Chapter 5: Optimizing Your Website for Success

- Basics of on-page SEO: Title tags, meta descriptions, and headers.
- Mobile-first indexing and site speed optimization.

- Example: A local gym improving its website and increasing memberships.

Chapter 6: Creating Content That Converts

- Types of content small businesses should focus on (blogs, videos, infographics).
- Storytelling techniques to make content engaging.
- Checklist: Steps to create and publish SEO-friendly content.

Chapter 7: The Importance of Backlinks for Credibility

- Understanding backlinks and why they matter.
- Simple strategies for small businesses to earn quality backlinks.
- Actionable tip: Building partnerships with local bloggers and influencers.

Chapter 8: Social Media Marketing and SEO: A Perfect Pair

- How social media supports SEO efforts.
- Tips for crafting shareable posts and driving traffic to your website.
- Checklist: Daily and weekly social media SEO integration tasks.

Chapter 9: Reviews and Reputation: Winning Customers' Trust

- The impact of reviews on local SEO rankings.

- Encouraging customers to leave positive reviews.
- Example: A repair shop leveraging reviews to gain new customers.

Chapter 10: Leveraging Analytics to Track Progress

- Introduction to Google Analytics and Search Console for small businesses.
- Key metrics to monitor and interpret.
- Actionable tips: Using analytics to refine your SEO strategy.

Chapter 11: The Role of Video in SEO

- Why video content is dominating SEO in 2024.
- How to create simple, impactful videos for your business.
- Example: A pet groomer using videos to grow local awareness.

Chapter 12: The Future of Voice Search

- How voice search is reshaping SEO for small businesses.
- Tips for optimizing content for voice queries.
- Checklist: Making your website voice-search friendly.

Chapter 13: Seasonal SEO and Marketing Strategies

- Tying SEO efforts to holiday and seasonal trends.
- Creating seasonal content that drives traffic.

- Example: A florist attracting Valentine's Day customers through SEO.

Chapter 14: Email Marketing and SEO Synergy

- How email marketing can amplify your SEO strategy.
- Examples of integrating keywords and links in email campaigns.
- Checklist: Building an SEO-friendly email newsletter.

Chapter 15: Managing Your SEO Budget Wisely

- Affordable tools and services for small business SEO.
- Free versus paid resources: What's worth investing in?
- Actionable tips: Prioritizing your SEO efforts based on your budget.

Chapter 16: Avoiding SEO Pitfalls and Mistakes

- Common mistakes small business owners make in SEO.
- How to stay compliant with search engine guidelines.
- Checklist: Red flags to avoid in your SEO strategy.

Chapter 17: Staying Motivated and Consistent

- The importance of patience and persistence in SEO.
- Inspirational case studies of small businesses thriving through long-term SEO.

- Final checklist: Your 12-month SEO roadmap.

Introduction: New Year, New Opportunities

The start of a new year is more than just a turn of the calendar—it's an invitation for fresh opportunities, bold ambitions, and meaningful change. For small business owners, the New Year offers a chance to reflect on past successes and challenges, recalibrate strategies, and set the stage for a year of growth. One of the most powerful ways to embrace this renewal is by refining your approach to online visibility through search engine optimization (SEO).

SEO can feel intimidating, especially when you're juggling the countless responsibilities of running a business. Maybe you've dabbled in SEO before, or perhaps it's a term you've only heard in passing. Either way, this book is here to demystify SEO, making it approachable, actionable, and tailored specifically for small businesses like yours.

Why SEO Matters Now More Than Ever

In today's digital age, customers are turning to search engines to find everything from their next meal to their local mechanic. If your business isn't showing up where potential customers are looking, you're leaving money on the table. SEO isn't just a buzzword; it's a fundamental pillar of marketing that can make your business more discoverable, trusted, and competitive.

The beauty of SEO is its ability to level the playing field. You don't need the marketing budget of a Fortune 500 company to succeed. Instead, by focusing on smart, targeted strategies, you can carve out a significant online presence that resonates with your local community and beyond.

This Book Is Your Roadmap

"New Year's SEO Resolutions for Your Business" is designed to guide you step-by-step through practical SEO strategies that you can implement today. Each chapter focuses on a specific aspect of SEO and digital marketing, breaking it down into manageable actions with real-life examples and checklists. Whether you're optimizing your website, building local authority, or enhancing your social media game, this book offers actionable advice tailored to your needs as a small business owner.

What You'll Learn

This book will teach you how to:

- Identify and implement SEO goals that align with your business objectives.
- Optimize your website to rank higher on search engines and attract more customers.
- Leverage local SEO to connect with your community and increase foot traffic.
- Create content that not only engages but also converts readers into loyal customers.
- Harness the power of social media and email marketing to amplify your online presence.
- Track and measure your progress to ensure your efforts are paying off.

Each chapter concludes with actionable checklists and tips, ensuring you can put what you've learned into practice immediately.

A Practical and Inspirational Approach

SEO is more than just a technical task—it's an opportunity to connect with your audience in meaningful ways. By the end of this book, you'll not only have the tools to improve your search rankings but also the confidence to approach your marketing with clarity and purpose.

The New Year is a blank slate, full of untapped potential. By committing to these SEO resolutions, you're not just improving your online presence—you're building a stronger, more resilient foundation for your business's success.

Let's get started.

Chapter 1: New Year, New Opportunities:

Why SEO Matters for Small Businesses

The New Year Mindset

January is a time of possibilities, brimming with enthusiasm to turn over a new leaf and achieve new goals. For small business owners, the question isn't *if* this should be a year of growth but *how* that growth will be realized. Amidst goals of increasing revenue, attracting new customers, and expanding your brand's reach, one strategy reigns supreme: enhancing your online visibility through SEO.

Search engine optimization is not just for big corporations with massive budgets. In fact, small businesses have a unique advantage in this space. By focusing on local SEO, creating targeted content, and leveraging your authentic connection to your community, you can position yourself as a trusted authority in your industry.

What SEO Brings to the Table

The days of relying solely on traditional advertising to reach customers are long gone. Your audience has shifted to online platforms, where searches are their first step toward finding solutions. Whether someone is looking for "the best coffee shop near me" or "reliable car repairs in [city]," the businesses that rank at the top of search results reap the rewards of visibility.

SEO ensures your business gets found when it matters most. It:

1. **Increases Discoverability**: Potential customers are actively searching for your products or services online. SEO helps your business appear in their search results.

2. **Builds Credibility**: A higher search ranking signals trust and authority to potential customers.

3. **Drives Relevant Traffic**: SEO targets users who are already interested in what you offer, ensuring the visitors you attract are likely to convert.

4. **Supports Long-Term Growth**: Unlike paid ads, the benefits of good SEO compound over time, making it a sustainable investment.

Small Businesses Winning with SEO: Real-Life Examples

Let's look at how small businesses have leveraged SEO to transform their presence:

- **The Local Cafe's Rise**
  A small-town cafe struggled with foot traffic, even during peak hours. By optimizing their Google Business Profile and creating blog posts around phrases like "best coffee in [town]" and "family-friendly cafes near me," they not only attracted tourists but also gained loyal local patrons.

- **The Handmade Jewelry Brand**
  A small handmade jewelry business wanted to stand out in a crowded market. By researching keywords like "unique handmade necklaces" and "artisan jewelry in [state]," they optimized their product descriptions and blog content. Over six months, organic traffic to their website tripled, and their online sales skyrocketed.

These businesses didn't have massive budgets. What they had was determination, focus, and a willingness to implement actionable SEO strategies.

SEO as a Competitive Advantage

Small businesses are often deeply connected to their local communities. This gives them a natural edge in local SEO, which focuses on geographical relevance. With tools like Google Business Profile, localized keywords, and review management, small businesses can easily compete against larger brands within their niche.

Your Action Plan for January

Here's how to start incorporating SEO into your business strategy this month:

1. **Audit Your Online Presence**
    - Search for your business online and assess where and how it appears in search results.
    - Check your Google Business Profile and ensure all details are accurate (address, hours, services, etc.).

2. **Set SEO Goals**
    - Identify specific outcomes you want from your SEO efforts. Examples: "Increase website traffic by 20%," "Gain 10 new customer reviews this month," or "Rank in the top 3 for [local keyword]."

3. **Claim Your Local Listings**
    - Ensure your business is listed on platforms like Yelp, Bing Places, and Apple Maps in addition to Google.

4. **Focus on Mobile Optimization**

- Over 60% of searches come from mobile devices. Make sure your website is mobile-friendly and loads quickly.

Checklist: Start Your SEO Journey Today

- Claim or update your Google Business Profile.
- Conduct a quick audit of your website, focusing on user experience.
- Brainstorm three local keywords relevant to your business.
- Encourage loyal customers to leave online reviews.
- Set one measurable SEO goal for the first quarter of the year.

SEO isn't about achieving everything all at once—it's about consistent, small steps that add up to significant progress. By starting now, you're setting your business up for a year of growth, visibility, and success.

Chapter 2: Setting Goals for SEO Success

Why Goals Matter in SEO

Every successful journey begins with a clear destination. When it comes to SEO, having well-defined goals is essential for measuring progress and staying motivated. Without them, you risk investing time and resources without knowing whether your efforts are paying off.

For small business owners, SEO goals should align with your overall business objectives. Are you aiming to attract more local customers? Do you want to increase online sales or build your email list? Defining your goals will guide your strategy and ensure you focus on the areas that matter most.

The SMART Framework for SEO Goals

The SMART framework is a proven method for setting effective goals. Let's break it down and apply it to SEO:

1. **Specific**: Clearly state what you want to achieve.

- Example: "Increase my website's organic traffic by 25% over the next six months."

2. **Measurable**: Ensure your goal can be quantified and tracked.
   - Example: Track website visits, leads generated, or keyword rankings.
3. **Achievable**: Set a realistic target based on your resources and starting point.
   - Example: If you're just starting, focus on improving rankings for local keywords instead of competing for high-volume national terms.
4. **Relevant**: Your goal should align with your business objectives.
   - Example: A local bakery might focus on driving foot traffic rather than nationwide e-commerce sales.
5. **Time-bound**: Set a deadline for achieving your goal.
   - Example: "Achieve my traffic increase by June 30th, 2024."

Breaking Down Common SEO Goals for Small Businesses

Here are some practical SEO goals to consider based on your business needs:

1. **Increase Local Visibility**
   - Goal: Appear in the top 3 results for "[your service] near me."

- Strategy: Optimize your Google Business Profile, use localized keywords, and build backlinks from local websites.

2. **Drive More Website Traffic**

    - Goal: Boost monthly organic visits by 20%.
    - Strategy: Publish SEO-friendly blog posts targeting customer questions and trending topics.

3. **Improve Conversion Rates**

    - Goal: Convert 10% of website visitors into leads or customers.
    - Strategy: Optimize landing pages, improve calls to action, and streamline the user experience.

4. **Build Brand Authority**

    - Goal: Earn backlinks from 5 reputable websites in your industry.
    - Strategy: Pitch guest blog posts, collaborate with local influencers, and create shareable content.

Practical Example: Goal Setting in Action

Imagine you own a small landscaping business. You've noticed that most of your competitors show up on the first page of search results for terms like "lawn care in [city]" or "affordable landscapers near me," but your website is buried on page three.

Here's how you could use SMART goals:

- **Specific**: "Rank on the first page of Google for the keyword 'lawn care in [city].'"

- **Measurable**: Track your ranking weekly using tools like SEMrush or Google Search Console.
- **Achievable**: Commit to optimizing your website's content and earning at least five backlinks from local sources.
- **Relevant**: Improved rankings directly impact your goal of increasing local leads.
- **Time-bound**: "Achieve this by April 1st, 2024."

Building an SEO Roadmap

Once you've set your goals, it's time to create a roadmap outlining the specific steps you'll take to achieve them. Here's an example:

Month 1:

- Conduct a website audit to identify technical SEO issues.
- Perform keyword research to discover terms your customers are searching for.

Month 2:

- Optimize your website's meta titles, descriptions, and headers with the selected keywords.
- Update your Google Business Profile with fresh images and posts.

Month 3:

- Publish two blog posts targeting local search queries (e.g., "How to Maintain a Healthy Lawn in [city]").
- Reach out to local bloggers or business directories for backlink opportunities.

Common Pitfalls to Avoid

1. **Setting Unrealistic Goals**: It's tempting to aim for the moon, but remember that SEO takes time. Start with manageable milestones.

2. **Ignoring Metrics**: Without tracking your performance, you won't know what's working or where to improve.

3. **Focusing Solely on Rankings**: While rankings are important, they're not the only measure of success. Pay attention to website traffic, engagement, and conversions.

Checklist: Define Your SEO Goals Today

- Write down one SMART SEO goal for the next quarter.
- Identify three keywords you want to rank for.
- Outline a simple three-month action plan.
- Choose a tool (e.g., Google Analytics, Search Console) to track your progress.
- Commit to reviewing your results monthly and adjusting your strategy as needed.

SEO success starts with clarity. By defining your goals now, you'll lay a solid foundation for all the strategies and actions covered in the upcoming chapters.

Chapter 3: Local SEO:

Capturing Your Community's Attention

What Is Local SEO and Why Does It Matter?

For small businesses, the community is your foundation. Your customers aren't just numbers on a website—they're neighbors, friends, and locals who share the same city streets. Local SEO focuses on helping your business show up in search results when someone searches for services or products nearby.

Consider this: over 46% of all Google searches are seeking local information. If your business isn't optimized for local SEO, you're missing out on a massive opportunity to connect with potential customers.

Key Components of Local SEO

1. **Google Business Profile**
   Your Google Business Profile (GBP) is the cornerstone of local SEO. This free tool allows your business to appear on Google Maps, in the Local Pack (the top three results), and in Knowledge Panels.
   - Actionable Tip: Ensure your profile is fully filled out, including your address, hours, phone number, services, and high-quality images.

2. **Local Keywords**
   Local keywords combine search terms with geographical locations. For example: "plumber in Dallas" or "organic groceries near me."
   - Actionable Tip: Use tools like Google's Keyword Planner or Ubersuggest to discover what your customers are searching for locally.

3. **Online Reviews**
   Reviews are not only a trust signal for potential customers but also influence your local search rankings.
   - Actionable Tip: Encourage satisfied customers to leave positive reviews on Google and other review platforms.

4. **Local Backlinks**
   Backlinks from other local websites, such as community blogs or local news outlets, can significantly boost your local SEO.
   - Actionable Tip: Reach out to local partners for collaborations or sponsorships that include backlinks.

5. **NAP Consistency**
   NAP stands for Name, Address, and Phone Number. These details should be consistent across all platforms, from your website to your GBP to social media.
   - Actionable Tip: Regularly audit your business listings to ensure consistency.

A Step-by-Step Guide to Mastering Local SEO

Step 1: Claim and Optimize Your Google Business Profile

- Log into your Google account and claim your business listing.
- Add complete and accurate information.
- Post regular updates, such as promotions, events, or new services.

Step 2: Perform a Local SEO Audit

- Search for your business on Google and see how it appears.
- Check your ranking for local keywords.
- Review competitors' GBP listings to identify gaps or opportunities.

Step 3: Incorporate Local Keywords

- Use local keywords in your website's meta titles, meta descriptions, and headers.
- Create content that addresses specific local questions, such as "Best family-friendly restaurants in [city]."

Step 4: Build Local Citations

- Ensure your business is listed on local directories, such as Yelp, Yellow Pages, and niche-specific platforms.

Step 5: Gather Reviews

- Politely ask satisfied customers to leave reviews, either in person or via follow-up emails.
- Respond to all reviews—positive and negative—to show you value customer feedback.

Real-Life Example: A Local Business Winning with SEO

Imagine a small bookstore in a bustling downtown area. Before focusing on local SEO, they relied solely on foot traffic. By optimizing their Google Business Profile, adding photos of their store, and posting weekly updates about new arrivals and events, they saw a 30% increase in walk-in customers.

Additionally, they wrote a blog series titled "Hidden Gems in [City]" that featured local attractions, which helped them rank for searches like "unique things to do in [city]." The result? More visibility, higher engagement, and a stronger connection with the community.

Mistakes to Avoid in Local SEO

1. **Ignoring Your Google Business Profile**
   A neglected profile can hurt your rankings and drive customers to competitors.

2. **Overlooking Negative Reviews**
   Failing to address customer complaints can damage your reputation.

3. **Keyword Stuffing**
   Using keywords unnaturally can lead to penalties and alienate readers.

Checklist: Your Local SEO Action Plan

- Claim or update your Google Business Profile.
- Research three local keywords relevant to your business.
- Optimize your website for local search terms.
- Ensure NAP consistency across all platforms.
- Build at least two new local backlinks this month.
- Respond to all existing customer reviews.

Local SEO is the bridge between your business and your community. By focusing on this aspect of search optimization, you're not just improving your visibility—you're strengthening your presence as a trusted, reliable part of the local landscape.

Chapter 4: The Power of Keywords: Speaking Your Customers' Language

Understanding the Role of Keywords

Keywords are the foundation of SEO. These are the phrases and terms that potential customers type into search engines to find businesses, products, and services like yours. When your website and online content align with these keywords, search engines are more likely to connect your business with the people who need it.

For small businesses, choosing the right keywords is critical. You don't need to compete with national or global brands for high-competition terms. Instead, focus on what your customers are searching for locally and specifically. This targeted approach saves time, money, and effort while delivering better results.

How Keywords Impact SEO

1. **Improved Visibility**
   Using relevant keywords increases your chances of appearing in search results when customers look for your services.

2. **Targeted Traffic**
   The right keywords attract visitors who are more likely to convert into customers.

3. **Increased Engagement**
   Content that matches customer searches feels more relevant and useful, keeping visitors on your site longer.

Types of Keywords to Focus On

1. **Short-Tail Keywords**
   These are broad terms with high search volume but high competition, like "plumber" or "coffee shop." Small businesses typically find these less effective.

2. **Long-Tail Keywords**
   Longer, more specific phrases like "24-hour plumber in [city]" or "best organic coffee near me." These have lower competition and are ideal for small businesses.

3. **Local Keywords**
   Phrases that include a geographic element, such as "[service] in [city]" or "near me" searches.

4. **Transactional Keywords**
   Keywords that indicate purchase intent, such as "buy," "order," or "book now."

How to Research Keywords

Step 1: Brainstorm Customer Questions

Think about what your customers might ask when searching for your business. For example:

- "Where can I find affordable lawn care in [city]?"
- "Best Italian restaurant near me."

Step 2: Use Keyword Research Tools

There are many tools available to help you find relevant keywords:

- **Free Tools**: Google Keyword Planner, Ubersuggest, Answer the Public.
- **Paid Tools**: SEMrush, Ahrefs, Moz.

Step 3: Analyze the Competition
Look at competitors' websites to see which keywords they're targeting. This can inspire new ideas and help you identify gaps.

Step 4: Prioritize Relevance and Volume
Choose keywords that balance search volume with relevance to your business. It's better to rank highly for a niche term than be buried in a broad, competitive category.

Optimizing Your Website with Keywords

1. **Title Tags and Meta Descriptions**
    - Place primary keywords in your title tags and meta descriptions to tell search engines what your page is about.

2. **Headers and Subheaders**
    - Use keywords naturally in headers (H1, H2, etc.) to improve readability and SEO.

3. **Content**
    - Create blog posts, FAQs, and service pages that include your target keywords. Keep the content valuable and avoid keyword stuffing.

4. **URLs**
    - Include keywords in your URLs for better indexing. Example: "www.example.com/best-lawn-care-dallas."

5. **Image Alt Text**
    - Use keywords in image descriptions to enhance accessibility and SEO.

Example: Targeting Keywords in Action

Imagine you own a pet grooming business in Denver. Instead of targeting "pet grooming" (a high-competition term), focus on:

- "Affordable dog grooming in Denver."
- "Cat grooming services near me."

You create a blog post titled "5 Tips for Keeping Your Dog's Coat Healthy in Denver Winters" and optimize it with these keywords. Over time, your site starts ranking higher for local searches, driving more traffic and leads.

Common Keyword Mistakes to Avoid

1. **Keyword Stuffing**
   Repeating the same keyword excessively can lead to penalties and make your content hard to read.

2. **Ignoring Search Intent**
   Make sure the keywords match what the user is looking for. A blog about "best budget laptops" won't satisfy someone searching for "luxury laptops."

3. **Neglecting Long-Tail Keywords**
   Small businesses often overlook these, despite their effectiveness in attracting niche audiences.

Checklist: Get Started with Keywords Today

- Brainstorm 5-10 phrases your customers might search for.
- Use a keyword research tool to refine your list.
- Create one piece of content around a long-tail keyword.
- Optimize your homepage with your primary keyword.
- Audit your current website for opportunities to add or refine keywords.

Keywords are the language of your customers. By speaking their language, you're not only improving your visibility but also creating a connection that leads to trust and loyalty.

Chapter 5: Optimizing Your Website for Success

Why Website Optimization Matters

Your website is the digital storefront of your business. Even if your SEO efforts bring visitors to your site, poor user experience (UX), slow loading times, or outdated design can drive them away. Optimizing your website ensures that the visitors you attract stay engaged, explore your offerings, and take the desired actions, whether it's making a purchase, booking a service, or contacting you for more information.

A well-optimized website doesn't just please your customers; it also signals to search engines that your site is trustworthy, relevant, and worth ranking higher.

Key Elements of Website Optimization

1. **User Experience (UX)**
   - A user-friendly website encourages visitors to stay longer and interact more.
   - Actionable Tip: Test your website's navigation. Can users easily find what they're looking for?

2. **Mobile-Friendliness**
   - Over 60% of searches come from mobile devices, so your site must work seamlessly on smaller screens.
   - Actionable Tip: Use Google's Mobile-Friendly Test tool to check your website's compatibility.

3. **Site Speed**
   - Slow loading times can frustrate visitors and negatively impact your rankings.
   - Actionable Tip: Use tools like PageSpeed Insights or GTmetrix to identify speed issues and fix them.

4. **On-Page SEO**
   - Optimizing individual pages for keywords helps search engines understand your content.
   - Actionable Tip: Use keywords naturally in titles, headers, and throughout your content.

5. **Clear Calls-to-Action (CTAs)**
   - A CTA guides visitors to take the next step, such as "Book Now," "Learn More," or "Contact Us."
   - Actionable Tip: Place CTAs prominently on every page.

Step-by-Step Guide to Website Optimization

Step 1: Audit Your Website

- Start by reviewing your website for common issues like broken links, outdated content, and missing images.
- Use tools like Screaming Frog or SEMrush for a detailed audit.

Step 2: Improve Page Load Times

- Compress large images using tools like TinyPNG.
- Minimize unnecessary scripts or plugins that slow your site.
- Use a Content Delivery Network (CDN) to deliver content faster.

Step 3: Optimize for Mobile Users

- Ensure that text is readable without zooming.
- Use responsive design to adapt your site to different screen sizes.
- Test all buttons and forms to ensure they work on touchscreens.

Step 4: Enhance On-Page SEO

- Include your primary keyword in:
    - The page title and meta description.
    - The first 100 words of your content.
    - At least one header (H1 or H2).
- Add internal links to guide users to related content.

Step 5: Improve Website Structure

- Organize your pages logically. For example:
    - Homepage → Services → Individual Service Pages.
- Use a simple, intuitive menu structure.

Real-Life Example: The Power of Optimization

A small boutique hotel in Savannah, Georgia, wanted to attract more direct bookings through its website. After optimizing their site's speed, updating the mobile experience, and adding CTAs like "Book Your Stay Today," they noticed a 40% increase in direct reservations within three months. They also created dedicated landing pages for specific keywords like "romantic getaways in Savannah," which improved their rankings and drove more organic traffic.

Common Website Optimization Mistakes

1. **Neglecting Mobile Users**
    - A site that looks great on desktop but doesn't work on mobile will lose a significant portion of potential customers.

2. **Ignoring Security**
    - Not having an SSL certificate (HTTPS) can lower trust and hurt rankings.

3. **Overloading Pages**
    - Too many images, videos, or widgets can slow down your site and overwhelm visitors.

4. **Using Generic CTAs**
    - CTAs like "Click Here" don't tell visitors what to expect or why they should take action.

Checklist: Optimize Your Website Today

- Perform a full website audit using an SEO tool.
- Compress and optimize all images for faster loading.
- Test your website on mobile devices to ensure compatibility.
- Add relevant keywords to your meta titles, descriptions, and content.
- Ensure every page includes a clear, compelling CTA.
- Organize your site's structure to make navigation easy.
- Check your site's security by ensuring you have an SSL certificate.

A well-optimized website is the foundation for any successful SEO strategy. It not only attracts visitors but also keeps them engaged and ready to take action.

Chapter 6: Creating Content That Converts

Why Content Is Key to SEO

"Content is king" may sound like a cliché, but it remains true in the world of SEO. Content is how you communicate with your audience, showcase your expertise, and guide potential customers through their buying journey. High-quality, targeted content not only drives traffic to your website but also builds trust, engages visitors, and turns them into loyal customers.

For small businesses, creating the right content is less about volume and more about delivering value. By addressing your audience's needs, answering their questions, and solving their problems, you position yourself as the go-to resource in your niche.

Types of Content to Focus On

1. **Blog Posts**
    - Ideal for answering common customer questions and providing helpful tips.
    - Example: A bakery writing a blog titled "5 Tips for Perfect Holiday Cookies."

2. **Landing Pages**
    - These are specific pages designed to convert visitors by focusing on a single topic or service.
    - Example: A plumber creating a landing page for "Emergency Plumbing Services in [City]."

3. **Videos**
    - Engaging and shareable, videos are perfect for tutorials, product demos, or testimonials.
    - Example: A fitness studio sharing workout videos for beginners.

4. **FAQs**
    - Answering frequently asked questions builds trust and improves your chances of appearing in voice search results.
    - Example: A law firm creating an FAQ section about common legal issues.

5. **Infographics**
    - Visual content is highly shareable and easy to understand.
    - Example: A car repair shop creating an infographic titled "Signs Your Car Needs a Tune-Up."

The Anatomy of Content That Converts

1. **Attention-Grabbing Headlines**
    - Your headline is the first thing readers see, so make it compelling and keyword-rich.
    - Example: "Top 10 Ways to Save Money on Home Repairs in [City]."

2. **Value-Driven Content**
    - Focus on solving problems, providing actionable tips, or offering unique insights.

3. **Engaging Visuals**
    - Use images, videos, or graphics to break up text and make content more engaging.

4. **Clear Calls-to-Action (CTAs)**

- Every piece of content should include a next step, such as "Contact us for more information" or "Download our free guide."

5. **SEO Optimization**
    - Use your target keywords naturally throughout the content, including headers, meta descriptions, and image alt text.

How to Create SEO-Friendly Content

Step 1: Understand Your Audience

- Identify your target customers' pain points, interests, and frequently asked questions.
- Use tools like Google Trends, Answer the Public, and social media polls to gather insights.

Step 2: Perform Keyword Research

- Choose one primary keyword and a few secondary keywords for each piece of content.
- Ensure the keywords align with your audience's intent.

Step 3: Plan Your Content

- Outline your content to ensure it flows logically.
- Include an introduction, main points, and a conclusion with a clear CTA.

Step 4: Write with Clarity and Purpose

- Avoid jargon and keep sentences concise.
- Write as if you're having a conversation with your audience.

Step 5: Optimize for Search Engines

- Include your primary keyword in the title, first paragraph, headers, and conclusion.
- Add internal and external links to boost credibility and navigation.

Step 6: Promote Your Content

- Share your content on social media, via email newsletters, and in online communities.
- Encourage readers to comment, share, or ask questions.

Real-Life Example: Content That Converts

A small accounting firm wanted to attract more local clients during tax season. They created a blog post titled "5 Tax Deductions Every Small Business Owner in [City] Should Know." The post included practical advice, easy-to-understand examples, and a CTA encouraging readers to schedule a free consultation.

The results? The blog ranked on the first page for "small business tax help in [City]," brought in significant website traffic, and generated 15 new client inquiries within a month.

Common Content Mistakes to Avoid

1. **Creating Generic Content**
   - Content that doesn't offer unique value won't engage readers or rank well.
2. **Keyword Stuffing**

- Overusing keywords makes content unnatural and can lead to penalties.

3. **Ignoring Formatting**

    - Long blocks of text without headers or visuals are harder to read and less engaging.

4. **Neglecting the CTA**

    - Content without a clear next step is a missed opportunity.

Checklist: Start Creating High-Converting Content Today

- Identify 3-5 topics that address your audience's needs or interests.
- Perform keyword research for each topic.
- Write one piece of content using an outline and include a clear CTA.
- Add visuals (images, videos, or infographics) to enhance the content.
- Share your content on at least two promotional platforms.

Content is more than just words on a page—it's your opportunity to connect, inspire, and convert. By creating valuable, engaging content tailored to your audience, you're not just improving your SEO but also building a loyal customer base.

Chapter 7: The Importance of Backlinks for Credibility

What Are Backlinks and Why Do They Matter?

Backlinks, also known as inbound or incoming links, are links from other websites that point to your own. Think of them as votes of confidence: when a reputable website links to your business, it signals to search engines that your content is valuable, trustworthy, and worth ranking higher.

For small businesses, backlinks can significantly boost your credibility, increase website traffic, and improve your SEO performance. However, the focus should always be on quality over quantity. A few links from high-authority sites are far more valuable than dozens of links from irrelevant or spammy sources.

How Backlinks Impact SEO

1. **Increased Search Rankings**
   Search engines view backlinks as endorsements. The more high-quality backlinks your site has, the higher it's likely to rank in search results.

2. **More Referral Traffic**
   Visitors who click on backlinks to your site are often highly interested in your content, products, or services.

3. **Enhanced Credibility**
   Being linked by reputable sources increases your authority in your industry, both with search engines and potential customers.

Types of Backlinks to Pursue

1. **Editorial Backlinks**
    - These are links earned when your content is referenced in a blog post, news article, or guide.
    - Example: A local newspaper linking to your business in an article about top-rated cafes.

2. **Guest Post Links**
    - Writing guest articles for other websites often includes a backlink to your own site.

- 3. **Local Backlinks**
    - Links from local directories, community websites, or business associations.
    - Example: A link from your city's Chamber of Commerce website.
- 4. **Social Mentions**
    - While not as impactful as direct backlinks, mentions and links on social media can still drive traffic and boost visibility.

How to Build Backlinks for Your Business

Step 1: Create High-Quality, Shareable Content

- Focus on producing content that others naturally want to link to.
- Examples: How-to guides, industry reports, infographics, and case studies.

Step 2: Reach Out to Local Partners

- Collaborate with other small businesses, nonprofits, or influencers in your area.
- Example: Sponsor a community event and request a link to your website from the event's page.

Step 3: Pitch to Local Bloggers or Journalists

- Share your expertise or business story with local bloggers or news outlets.
- Example: Offer an interview or provide data for a story they're covering.

Step 4: Leverage Directories and Listings

- Ensure your business is listed in relevant directories like Yelp, TripAdvisor, or industry-specific platforms.

Step 5: Monitor Your Backlinks

- Use tools like Ahrefs, SEMrush, or Moz to keep track of who's linking to your site. This helps identify opportunities for more backlinks or address harmful links.

Real-Life Example: A Small Business Growing Through Backlinks

A local yoga studio wanted to expand its customer base and increase its online presence. They wrote an in-depth blog post titled "5 Health Benefits of Yoga for Busy Professionals" and shared it with a local health and wellness blog. The blog not only linked back to the yoga studio's website but also featured an interview with the studio's owner.

The result? The backlink from the health blog drove targeted traffic to the studio's website, and the exposure boosted sign-ups for their beginner classes.

Common Backlink Pitfalls to Avoid

1. **Buying Links**
    - Paid links from low-quality sites can lead to penalties from search engines.

2. **Focusing on Quantity Over Quality**
   - A few authoritative links are more impactful than dozens of irrelevant ones.

3. **Ignoring Broken Links**
   - Missed opportunities: Reach out to websites linking to outdated or broken content and suggest your content as a replacement.

4. **Using Irrelevant Anchor Text**
   - The clickable text of a link (anchor text) should be relevant to the content it points to.

Checklist: Start Building Backlinks Today

- Create one high-quality piece of content designed for backlinks.
- Identify and reach out to 3-5 local bloggers, journalists, or businesses for collaboration.
- Submit your business to 3 relevant directories or industry listings.
- Monitor your backlinks using a tool like SEMrush or Moz.
- Replace broken links with your content where possible.

Backlinks are a critical part of SEO that builds your website's credibility and authority. By focusing on quality, collaboration, and value, you'll create a backlink profile that strengthens your search rankings and grows your online presence.

Chapter 8: Social Media Marketing and SEO:

A Perfect Pair

How Social Media Amplifies Your SEO Efforts

While social media doesn't directly impact search engine rankings, its role in supporting SEO is undeniable. Social media platforms help increase brand visibility, drive traffic to your website, and create opportunities for valuable backlinks. For small businesses, social media offers a cost-effective way to engage with your audience, build trust, and amplify your content.

The relationship between social media and SEO can be summed up as symbiotic: a strong social media presence boosts your SEO efforts, and well-optimized content attracts more social media engagement.

Key Benefits of Social Media for SEO

1. **Increased Traffic**
   Social media posts can drive users directly to your website, increasing traffic and engagement.

2. **Enhanced Content Sharing**
   When people share your content, it gains exposure and has a higher chance of earning backlinks.

3. **Improved Brand Awareness**
   A strong social media presence builds your brand's credibility, making users more likely to trust and visit your website.

4. **Supports Local SEO**
   Social platforms like Facebook and Instagram are powerful tools for engaging with your local audience.

Best Social Media Platforms for Small Businesses

1. **Facebook**
   - Ideal for community engagement, events, and sharing blog posts or promotions.
   - Features like Facebook Pages and Ads can help you reach a local audience effectively.

2. **Instagram**
   - Great for visual brands like retail, food, and lifestyle businesses.
   - Use hashtags and geotags to attract local followers.

3. **LinkedIn**
   - Perfect for B2B businesses or professional services looking to build authority and connections.

4. **Pinterest**
   - Useful for sharing how-to content, recipes, or design inspiration.

5. **Twitter**
   - Ideal for quick updates, sharing blog posts, and engaging in trending conversations.

How to Align Social Media and SEO

Step 1: Optimize Social Profiles

- Ensure your business profiles on platforms like Facebook and Instagram include your website link, contact information, and a brief, keyword-rich description.

Step 2: Share SEO-Optimized Content

- Share blog posts, guides, or videos that are optimized for SEO. Include an enticing caption and call-to-action to drive traffic back to your website.

Step 3: Use Local Hashtags and Tags

- For local businesses, hashtags like #YourCity and #LocalBusiness can increase discoverability.
- Tag local influencers or partner businesses to expand your reach.

Step 4: Encourage Social Sharing

- Add social sharing buttons to your blog posts and landing pages.
- Offer incentives for followers to share your content, such as giveaways or discounts.

Step 5: Leverage User-Generated Content

- Encourage customers to share photos or reviews of your products and tag your business.

Real-Life Example: Leveraging Social Media for SEO

A local florist wanted to increase website traffic and attract more customers for Valentine's Day. They created an Instagram campaign with posts featuring their top floral arrangements and used hashtags like #ValentinesFlowers and #BestFloristIn[City].

They also shared a blog post titled "5 Unique Valentine's Day Gift Ideas" on Facebook and included a link to their website. The result? Their website traffic doubled, and Valentine's Day orders increased by 35%.

Tips for Social Media Success

1. **Post Consistently**
   - Use scheduling tools like Buffer or Hootsuite to plan and maintain a steady stream of posts.

2. **Engage with Your Audience**
   - Respond to comments, messages, and reviews to build trust and loyalty.

3. **Experiment with Formats**
   - Test different types of content, such as videos, carousels, and live streams, to see what resonates most with your audience.

4. **Track Your Performance**
   - Use analytics tools provided by platforms to measure the reach, engagement, and traffic generated by your posts.

Common Social Media Mistakes to Avoid

1. **Focusing Solely on Followers**
   - A large follower count is meaningless if those followers aren't engaging with your content or visiting your website.

2. **Being Inconsistent**
    - Posting sporadically can make your audience forget about your brand.
3. **Over-Promoting**
    - Balance promotional posts with valuable, engaging content that resonates with your audience.

Checklist: Strengthen Your Social Media and SEO Connection Today

- Optimize your social media profiles with links and keywords.
- Share one SEO-optimized blog post or video on your platforms this week.
- Use at least three local hashtags in your next post.
- Encourage followers to share your content by offering an incentive.
- Monitor your social media analytics to identify what's driving the most traffic.

Social media is more than just a tool for engagement—it's a gateway to better SEO, increased website traffic, and stronger community connections. By aligning your social media strategy with your SEO goals, you'll create a powerful digital marketing ecosystem that supports your small business's growth.

Chapter 9: Reviews and Reputation: Winning Customers' Trust

The Power of Reviews in SEO

Online reviews are the modern equivalent of word-of-mouth marketing. Not only do they build trust and credibility with potential customers, but they also play a significant role in SEO. For small businesses, reviews are a golden opportunity to strengthen your reputation, attract local customers, and improve your search engine rankings.

Search engines like Google consider reviews as part of their ranking factors, especially for local SEO. Businesses with higher ratings and a larger volume of positive reviews are more likely to appear at the top of local search results, giving you a competitive edge.

How Reviews Influence SEO

1. **Improved Local Rankings**
   - Google prioritizes businesses with good reviews when displaying local results.
2. **Increased Click-Through Rates (CTR)**
   - Positive ratings and reviews make your business stand out in search results, encouraging users to click.
3. **Enhanced Trust**
   - Reviews act as social proof, convincing potential customers of your reliability and quality.

Where Reviews Matter Most

1. **Google Business Profile**
   - Reviews on your Google Business Profile have the most direct impact on local SEO.
2. **Industry-Specific Platforms**
   - Platforms like TripAdvisor, Yelp, or OpenTable are critical for businesses in specific niches like hospitality or dining.
3. **Social Media**

- Reviews and recommendations on Facebook can drive local engagement and visibility.

4. **Your Website**
   - Displaying customer testimonials or embedding review widgets can build credibility and keep visitors engaged.

How to Get More Reviews

Step 1: Ask at the Right Time

- Timing is everything. Request reviews shortly after a positive interaction, such as completing a service or making a sale.

Step 2: Make It Easy

- Provide direct links to your Google Business Profile or other review platforms.
- Include a simple request in follow-up emails or on receipts.

Step 3: Offer a Reminder Without Pressure

- Use signage in your store or office, such as "Love our service? Leave us a review!"

Step 4: Incentivize Reviews (Carefully)

- Offer small rewards, like a discount or entry into a giveaway, for leaving reviews—but ensure this complies with platform guidelines.

Step 5: Leverage Social Media

- Use posts or stories to encourage followers to share their experiences.

Responding to Reviews: The Good and the Bad

1. **Positive Reviews**
    - Respond promptly and thank the reviewer. Acknowledge their specific points to show your gratitude.
    - Example: "Thank you for your kind words, [Name]! We're thrilled to hear you loved our [product/service] and hope to see you again soon!"

2. **Negative Reviews**
    - Stay professional and avoid being defensive. Apologize for their experience and offer to resolve the issue offline.
    - Example: "We're sorry to hear about your experience, [Name]. Please contact us directly at [phone/email] so we can make things right."

3. **Neutral Reviews**
    - Use these as opportunities to ask for suggestions or feedback to improve your service.

Real-Life Example: Leveraging Reviews for Growth

A small cleaning service in Seattle struggled to compete with larger companies. By actively encouraging reviews, they went from 5 to 50 reviews on their Google Business Profile within six months.

They also responded to every review, thanking customers for their feedback and addressing any complaints professionally. As a result, they climbed to the top of Google's local search results for "cleaning services in Seattle," and their bookings increased by 60%.

Common Mistakes to Avoid

1. **Ignoring Reviews**
   - Failing to respond to reviews, especially negative ones, can harm your reputation.

2. **Faking Reviews**
   - Writing fake reviews or paying for them can lead to penalties and a loss of trust.

3. **Neglecting Platforms**
   - Don't focus solely on Google; reviews on other platforms matter too.

Checklist: Strengthen Your Reviews and Reputation Today

- Claim your business on review platforms like Google, Yelp, and industry-specific sites.
- Create a process to request reviews after positive customer interactions.
- Respond to all reviews—positive, neutral, or negative—promptly and professionally.
- Highlight your best reviews on your website or social media.
- Monitor your review profiles regularly to stay on top of feedback.

Reviews are a powerful tool for building trust, improving local SEO, and attracting new customers. By actively encouraging, responding to, and leveraging reviews, you're not only enhancing your online reputation but also setting your business apart from the competition.

Chapter 10: Leveraging Analytics to Track Progress

Why Analytics Are Crucial for SEO Success

SEO is not a one-time effort; it's an ongoing process of refinement and adjustment. The key to improving your SEO strategy is understanding what's working, what isn't, and how to optimize for better results. This is where analytics come in.

Analytics tools provide valuable insights into your website's performance, user behavior, and traffic sources. By leveraging this data, you can make informed decisions to maximize your efforts and achieve your business goals.

For small business owners, tracking analytics may seem daunting at first, but once you know what to look for, it becomes an indispensable part of your strategy.

The Most Important SEO Metrics to Track

1. **Organic Traffic**
   - Measures how many visitors arrive at your website through search engines.
   - Why It Matters: Increased organic traffic indicates better visibility in search results.

2. **Bounce Rate**

- The percentage of visitors who leave your site after viewing only one page.
- Why It Matters: A high bounce rate could signal poor user experience or irrelevant content.

3. **Session Duration**
    - The average time visitors spend on your site.
    - Why It Matters: Longer sessions often indicate engaging and useful content.

4. **Keyword Rankings**
    - Tracks how your target keywords are performing in search engine results.
    - Why It Matters: Higher rankings lead to greater visibility.

5. **Backlinks**
    - The number and quality of external sites linking to your website.
    - Why It Matters: Backlinks boost your credibility and authority.

6. **Click-Through Rate (CTR)**
    - The percentage of people who click your link after seeing it in search results.
    - Why It Matters: A higher CTR means your titles and meta descriptions are compelling.

7. **Conversion Rate**
    - The percentage of visitors who take a desired action (e.g., filling out a form, making a purchase).

- Why It Matters: It directly ties SEO efforts to your bottom line.

The Best Tools for Tracking Analytics

1. **Google Analytics**
   - Tracks website traffic, user behavior, and conversions.
   - Key Features: Real-time data, audience insights, and goal tracking.

2. **Google Search Console**
   - Monitors your website's presence in Google search results.
   - Key Features: Keyword rankings, index coverage, and performance reports.

3. **SEMrush or Ahrefs**
   - Comprehensive tools for tracking keywords, backlinks, and competitive analysis.

4. **Moz**
   - Focuses on keyword rankings and site audits.

5. **Hotjar**
   - Provides heatmaps and session recordings to understand user behavior.

How to Use Analytics to Improve Your SEO

Step 1: Set Up Your Tools

- Install Google Analytics and Google Search Console on your website.
- Create goals in Google Analytics to track specific actions, such as form submissions or purchases.

Step 2: Monitor Your Metrics Regularly

- Schedule weekly or monthly check-ins to review key metrics.
- Look for trends, such as increases in organic traffic or improvements in bounce rate.

Step 3: Identify What's Working

- Review your top-performing pages and keywords.
- Analyze what sets them apart—content quality, relevance, or user engagement—and replicate these strategies.

Step 4: Spot and Fix Issues

- High bounce rate on a particular page? Consider improving the content or optimizing the layout.
- Drop in rankings for a target keyword? Refresh the page with updated information and more internal links.

Step 5: Experiment and Optimize

- Use A/B testing to compare different headlines, CTAs, or layouts.
- Experiment with new content formats, such as videos or infographics, to see what drives engagement.

Real-Life Example: Analytics in Action

A small e-commerce store selling handmade candles noticed a drop in organic traffic. Using Google Analytics, they identified that their blog traffic had decreased, particularly for a popular post titled "Best Scents for Winter."

By analyzing Google Search Console, they saw that the keyword "winter candle scents" had fallen in rankings. They refreshed the blog post with updated content, optimized it with new internal links, and added a downloadable guide to encourage email sign-ups. Within a month, the post regained its rankings, and website traffic increased by 20%.

Common Analytics Mistakes to Avoid

1. **Ignoring the Data**
   - Collecting data without using it to inform decisions is a missed opportunity.

2. **Tracking Too Many Metrics**
   - Focus on actionable metrics that align with your business goals.

3. **Relying Solely on Tools**
   - Analytics tools provide insights, but human interpretation and strategic action are key.

4. **Making Snap Judgments**
   - SEO changes take time to show results. Avoid overreacting to short-term fluctuations.

Checklist: Start Tracking Your SEO Progress Today

- Set up Google Analytics and Google Search Console for your website.

- Identify 3-5 key metrics to monitor based on your goals.
- Review your top-performing pages and identify patterns.
- Investigate any pages with high bounce rates or low rankings.
- Use insights from analytics to adjust your strategy monthly.

Analytics are your window into the effectiveness of your SEO efforts. By regularly monitoring and interpreting your data, you can refine your strategy, maximize your ROI, and ensure that your business continues to grow.

Chapter 11: The Role of Video in SEO

Why Video Content is Dominating SEO

In today's digital landscape, video content has emerged as one of the most powerful tools for engaging audiences, driving traffic, and boosting SEO. Search engines prioritize websites with rich, diverse content, and video is a key player in that strategy. For small businesses, creating video content isn't just a trend—it's an opportunity to captivate your audience and elevate your SEO performance.

Consider this: video content is 50 times more likely to drive organic search results compared to plain text. With platforms like YouTube, Instagram, and TikTok leading the way, businesses that embrace video marketing are reaping the benefits of increased visibility and stronger connections with their audience.

How Videos Boost SEO

1. **Increased Engagement**
    - Videos keep visitors on your website longer, reducing bounce rates and signaling to search engines that your content is valuable.

2. **Higher Click-Through Rates (CTR)**
    - Thumbnails for videos in search results often attract more clicks than plain text links.

3. **Improved Backlink Potential**
    - High-quality videos are more likely to be shared and linked to by other websites.

4. **Enhanced Local SEO**
    - Video content can be optimized with local keywords to attract customers in your area.

5. **YouTube SEO**

- As the world's second-largest search engine, YouTube offers a unique opportunity to reach a massive audience.

Types of Videos Small Businesses Should Create

1. **Explainer Videos**
    - Showcase your products or services in a clear, engaging way.
    - Example: A bike repair shop creating a video titled "How to Fix a Flat Tire in 5 Minutes."

2. **Customer Testimonials**
    - Highlight satisfied customers sharing their positive experiences.

3. **Behind-the-Scenes Videos**
    - Give your audience a glimpse into your business operations, fostering trust and connection.

4. **Tutorials and How-Tos**
    - Teach your audience something valuable related to your niche.
    - Example: A bakery sharing "5 Easy Cake Decorating Tips."

5. **Promotional Videos**
    - Announce sales, events, or new product launches with short, attention-grabbing clips.

6. **Live Streams**

- Host Q&A sessions, product demonstrations, or behind-the-scenes events in real time.

How to Optimize Videos for SEO

Step 1: Choose the Right Keywords

- Perform keyword research to identify terms your audience searches for on YouTube and Google.
- Example: For a florist, keywords like "flower arrangement tutorial" or "how to keep flowers fresh longer" may be ideal.

Step 2: Write Compelling Titles and Descriptions

- Include your target keywords in video titles and descriptions.
- Example: "Beginner's Guide to Flower Arranging | Easy Steps for Stunning Bouquets."

Step 3: Add Transcripts

- Upload transcripts for your videos to make them accessible and help search engines understand the content.

Step 4: Use Tags and Categories

- Add relevant tags to your videos to increase discoverability.

Step 5: Optimize Thumbnails

- Create eye-catching thumbnails that encourage clicks.

Step 6: Embed Videos on Your Website

- Place videos on relevant pages of your website to enhance user experience and improve rankings.

Real-Life Example: Small Business Video Success

A local fitness studio wanted to attract more members. They created a series of videos on YouTube and Instagram, such as "10-Minute Home Workouts for Beginners" and "Stretching Tips to Prevent Injuries."

By optimizing these videos with local keywords like "fitness studio in [City]" and including a call-to-action for a free trial class, they saw a 40% increase in website traffic and gained 25 new memberships within two months.

Common Video SEO Mistakes to Avoid

1. **Neglecting Quality**
   - Poor lighting, audio, or editing can reduce the impact of your videos.

2. **Skipping Keywords**
   - Failing to include keywords in titles and descriptions limits your video's visibility.

3. **Ignoring Thumbnails**
   - A bland or irrelevant thumbnail can discourage clicks.

4. **Forgetting the CTA**
   - Always include a clear next step, such as visiting your website or subscribing to your channel.

Checklist: Start Creating SEO-Optimized Videos Today

- Identify 2-3 topics for your first set of videos.

- Perform keyword research to optimize titles and descriptions.
- Create a simple, visually appealing thumbnail for each video.
- Include transcripts to make your videos accessible.
- Share your videos on YouTube, social media, and your website.

Video content is a game-changer for small businesses looking to stand out online. By creating and optimizing engaging videos, you can connect with your audience on a deeper level, boost your SEO performance, and build a stronger digital presence.

Chapter 12: The Future of Voice Search

What Is Voice Search, and Why Does It Matter?

Voice search is rapidly changing the way people interact with search engines. With the rise of virtual assistants like Siri, Alexa, and Google Assistant, more consumers are asking questions and seeking answers through spoken commands rather than typing. For small businesses, this shift represents both a challenge and an opportunity to optimize for a growing trend.

Studies show that over 50% of online searches are now voice-based, and this number is expected to grow as smart devices become more popular. Voice search optimization is no longer optional—it's a critical part of staying ahead in the competitive SEO landscape.

How Voice Search Differs from Traditional Search

1. **Conversational Tone**
    - Voice searches are more conversational, often phrased as full questions or commands.
    - Example: Typing "best pizza near me" vs. asking "Where can I find the best pizza near me?"

2. **Focus on Local Searches**
   - Voice search often caters to local needs, such as finding nearby businesses or services.

3. **Long-Tail Keywords**
   - Voice queries tend to be longer and more specific than text searches.

4. **Mobile and On-the-Go Use**
   - Voice searches are frequently done on mobile devices or smart speakers, often when users need quick answers.

How Voice Search Impacts SEO

1. **Increased Importance of Local SEO**
   - Optimizing for phrases like "near me" or "open now" becomes critical.

2. **Rise of Featured Snippets**
   - Voice assistants often pull answers directly from featured snippets (position zero) on Google.

3. **Focus on Mobile-Friendly Websites**
   - Since many voice searches happen on mobile, a responsive, fast-loading website is essential.

How to Optimize Your Business for Voice Search

Step 1: Focus on Natural Language and Questions

- Write content in a conversational tone that mirrors how people speak.
- Example: Include FAQs like "What's the best way to clean carpets?" rather than only using generic headings like "Carpet Cleaning Tips."

Step 2: Prioritize Local SEO

- Ensure your Google Business Profile is updated with accurate details, including your address, phone number, and business hours.
- Use location-based keywords like "affordable haircuts in [City]."

Step 3: Target Long-Tail Keywords

- Research longer, more specific phrases that reflect voice queries.
- Example: Instead of "dentist," optimize for "family dentist accepting new patients in [City]."

Step 4: Improve Page Load Speed

- Voice search users expect instant answers, so a slow website can hurt your chances of ranking.

Step 5: Optimize for Featured Snippets

- Structure your content to answer questions clearly and concisely.
- Use bullet points, numbered lists, or short paragraphs to increase the chances of being featured.

Real-Life Example: Voice Search Optimization in Action

A small pest control company wanted to capture more local leads. By updating their website with an FAQ section, they included voice-friendly questions like "How do I get rid of ants in my kitchen?" They also optimized their Google Business Profile with keywords like "24-hour pest control in [City]."

Within three months, they saw a 25% increase in phone inquiries from customers using voice assistants like Alexa and Google Assistant.

Tips for Voice Search Success

1. **Answer Questions Directly**
   - Provide clear, concise answers within your content.

2. **Optimize for Mobile**
   - Ensure your website is mobile-friendly, fast, and easy to navigate.

3. **Focus on Local Optimization**
   - Add location-based keywords, and keep your Google Business Profile up to date.

4. **Use Structured Data Markup**
   - Schema markup helps search engines understand your content better and increases the likelihood of being featured in voice results.

Common Voice Search Mistakes to Avoid

1. **Ignoring Local SEO**

- Without local optimization, your business may not appear in relevant voice searches.

2. **Using Only Short Keywords**
    - Voice queries are longer, so relying solely on short-tail keywords limits your reach.

3. **Skipping Mobile Optimization**
    - A non-responsive or slow website won't rank well for voice searches.

Checklist: Prepare Your Business for Voice Search Today

- Create an FAQ page with natural-language questions and answers.
- Optimize your Google Business Profile with updated and accurate information.
- Use long-tail keywords that match conversational voice queries.
- Improve your website's mobile performance and page load speed.
- Structure your content to increase its chances of being featured in snippets.

Voice search isn't just a trend—it's the future of how customers will find businesses online. By optimizing your website and content for voice queries, you're positioning your business to meet the needs of today's on-the-go consumers while staying ahead in the evolving SEO landscape.

Chapter 13: Seasonal SEO and Marketing Strategies

Why Seasonal SEO Matters

Every business experiences seasonal trends, whether it's the back-to-school rush, the holiday shopping season, or summer tourism peaks. Seasonal SEO leverages these predictable patterns to capture your audience's attention when they're most likely to need your products or services.

For small businesses, seasonal SEO is a golden opportunity to align your marketing efforts with your customers' priorities and search habits. By preparing your website and content in advance, you can stay ahead of the competition and maximize traffic during peak seasons.

The Basics of Seasonal SEO

1. **Timing Is Everything**
    - Seasonal content should be created and published well before the peak period begins. For example, holiday shopping content should be ready by October.

2. **Keyword Research for Seasons**
    - Identify keywords that spike during certain times of the year, such as "Valentine's Day gifts" or "summer vacation deals."

3. **Focus on Relevant Content**
    - Tailor your content to match the needs of your audience during that season.

4. **Update Existing Content**
    - Refresh past seasonal content to keep it relevant and improve rankings.

How to Develop a Seasonal SEO Strategy

Step 1: Identify Seasonal Opportunities

- Review your business's past sales data and industry trends to pinpoint key seasonal periods.
- Example: A lawn care service could target "spring lawn maintenance tips" or "fall yard cleanup services."

Step 2: Perform Seasonal Keyword Research

- Use tools like Google Trends, SEMrush, or Answer the Public to identify trending search terms for your industry.
- Example: "Best Black Friday deals on [product]" or "Easter brunch in [city]."

Step 3: Create a Seasonal Content Calendar

- Map out when to create, publish, and promote seasonal content.
- Example: Start planning holiday content in August, publish it in October, and promote it through December.

Step 4: Optimize Landing Pages

- Create dedicated landing pages for seasonal campaigns with targeted keywords and strong calls-to-action.
- Example: "Book Your Thanksgiving Catering in [City] Today!"

Step 5: Promote Your Seasonal Content

- Share your content on social media, email newsletters, and local advertising channels.

Examples of Seasonal SEO in Action

1. **A Local Restaurant**
   - They create a blog post titled "Top 5 Holiday Catering Ideas in [City]" optimized with local keywords.
   - Results: Increased bookings for their catering services during the holiday season.

2. **An E-Commerce Store**
   - Launches a landing page for "Valentine's Day Gift Bundles" with a countdown timer to create urgency.
   - Results: Higher conversion rates and increased sales in February.

3. **A Fitness Studio**
   - Posts "New Year Fitness Challenges" on their website and promotes it with the keyword "Best gyms near me for New Year's resolutions."
   - Results: Boost in new memberships in January.

Tips for Successful Seasonal SEO

1. **Start Early**
   - Publish seasonal content 1-2 months before the peak period to allow search engines time to index it.

2. **Repurpose Content**
   - Update previous seasonal blog posts, landing pages, or promotions instead of starting from scratch.

3. **Leverage Social Media**

- Use social platforms to amplify your seasonal content and engage with customers in real time.

4. **Create a Sense of Urgency**
    - Use language like "limited-time offer" or "only a few spots left" to encourage action.

5. **Target Local Searches**
    - Include phrases like "near me" or your city name to attract nearby customers.

Common Mistakes to Avoid

1. **Publishing Too Late**
    - Seasonal content needs time to rank. Waiting until the last minute will reduce its effectiveness.

2. **Ignoring Local SEO**
    - Failing to optimize for local terms can mean missing out on nearby customers searching for seasonal services.

3. **Overloading Keywords**
    - Using too many keywords in a single piece of content can make it unreadable and hurt your rankings.

4. **Forgetting Post-Season Content**
    - After the season ends, update or repurpose the content for the next year.

Checklist: Prepare for Seasonal SEO Success

- Identify your business's top seasonal opportunities.
- Research and target trending seasonal keywords.
- Create a seasonal content calendar with publication dates.
- Optimize or update existing seasonal content.
- Promote your content through social media and email marketing.

Seasonal SEO is about being prepared and proactive. By aligning your content and marketing efforts with seasonal trends, you'll not only attract more traffic but also position your business as the go-to solution when your customers need it most.

Chapter 14: Email Marketing and SEO Synergy

Why Email Marketing and SEO Work Well Together

Email marketing and SEO might seem like separate strategies, but when combined, they create a powerful synergy that drives traffic, builds relationships, and boosts conversions. While SEO focuses on attracting potential customers through search engines, email marketing nurtures those leads by keeping them engaged and informed.

For small businesses, leveraging these two tools together can amplify your reach, strengthen your customer base, and maximize your marketing ROI.

How Email Marketing Supports SEO

1. **Driving Traffic to Your Website**
    - Sharing blog posts, product pages, or promotions in email campaigns encourages recipients to visit your website, increasing organic traffic.

2. **Boosting Engagement Metrics**
   - Email-driven visitors who spend time on your site, explore multiple pages, or convert signal to search engines that your content is valuable.
3. **Reusing SEO Content in Emails**
   - Repurposing blog posts or guides in email newsletters helps you get more mileage from your SEO efforts.
4. **Encouraging Backlinks**
   - Sending your content to industry contacts or loyal customers can lead to shares and backlinks, which improve your search rankings.

How SEO Supports Email Marketing

1. **Growing Your Email List**
   - Optimized landing pages and calls-to-action (CTAs) attract organic visitors and convert them into email subscribers.
2. **Creating Relevant Content**
   - SEO research helps you understand your audience's interests, enabling you to craft email campaigns that resonate.
3. **Improving Click-Through Rates**
   - Email campaigns that direct users to SEO-optimized content are more likely to achieve higher engagement.

Steps to Integrate Email Marketing and SEO

Step 1: Use SEO to Grow Your Email List

- Add email sign-up forms to high-traffic pages, such as blogs or service pages.
- Offer incentives like free guides, discounts, or exclusive content in exchange for email addresses.

Step 2: Share SEO Content Through Emails

- Include links to your blog posts, videos, or infographics in your newsletters.
- Use enticing subject lines to encourage clicks, such as "5 Ways to Save on [Service] This Winter."

Step 3: Create Targeted Campaigns

- Segment your email list based on interests or behavior to send personalized, SEO-aligned content.
- Example: If a customer downloaded a guide on home maintenance, send them an email featuring your "Top 10 DIY Home Repair Tips" blog.

Step 4: Track and Optimize Performance

- Use email analytics to monitor open rates, click-through rates, and website traffic from your campaigns.
- Refine your strategy by identifying which types of content perform best.

Examples of Email and SEO in Action

1. **E-Commerce Business**

- A clothing store creates a blog titled "5 Winter Wardrobe Essentials" optimized for seasonal keywords.
- They email the post to their subscribers, include links to featured products, and see a 20% increase in traffic and sales.

2. **Local Service Provider**
   - A plumber promotes their "Winter Plumbing Tips" blog post in an email campaign, attracting new clients during the colder months.
   - The blog ranks higher in search results due to increased traffic from the email campaign.

Best Practices for Email and SEO Integration

1. **Keep It Mobile-Friendly**
   - Ensure your emails and the content they link to are optimized for mobile devices.

2. **Write Engaging Subject Lines**
   - Treat subject lines like meta titles—make them concise, relevant, and enticing.

3. **Use Clear CTAs**
   - Guide recipients to your website with action-oriented language, such as "Read More," "Shop Now," or "Claim Your Discount."

4. **Test and Experiment**
   - A/B test your emails to determine which subject lines, content types, and designs work best.

Common Mistakes to Avoid

1. **Overloading Emails with Links**
   - Focus on 1-2 clear CTAs per email to avoid overwhelming recipients.

2. **Neglecting Segmentation**
   - Sending generic emails to your entire list may lead to lower engagement rates.

3. **Ignoring Analytics**
   - Failing to track performance metrics makes it harder to improve your strategy.

4. **Skipping Landing Page Optimization**
   - Ensure the pages your emails link to are optimized for both SEO and conversions.

Checklist: Align Your Email Marketing and SEO Today

- Add email sign-up forms to high-traffic pages on your website.
- Share at least one SEO-optimized blog post or guide in your next email campaign.
- Segment your email list to deliver personalized, relevant content.
- Use email analytics to track and refine your campaigns.
- Test subject lines and CTAs to maximize click-through rates.

Email marketing and SEO are better together. By integrating these two strategies, you'll create a seamless experience that attracts, engages, and converts your audience. This alignment ensures that your small business remains visible, relevant, and connected to your customers.

Chapter 15: Managing Your SEO Budget Wisely

Why Budget Management Matters for SEO

SEO is one of the most cost-effective marketing strategies for small businesses. Unlike paid ads, where visibility stops when you stop spending, SEO offers long-term value. However, it's essential to manage your budget wisely to maximize results and avoid wasting resources on unnecessary tools or ineffective strategies.

For small businesses with limited budgets, prioritizing the right efforts, tools, and services can make all the difference. This chapter will guide you in creating an SEO budget that works for your business, delivering the best ROI without breaking the bank.

What to Consider When Planning Your SEO Budget

1. **Your Business Goals**
   - Are you focused on increasing traffic, improving local visibility, or driving more conversions? Your budget should align with these goals.

2. **The Size of Your Website**
   - Larger websites with many pages may require a bigger budget for optimization.

3. **The Competitiveness of Your Industry**
   - Highly competitive industries may require more investment to outrank competitors.

4. **Your In-House Capabilities**

- Assess whether you have the skills to handle certain tasks yourself or need to outsource to professionals.

Where to Allocate Your SEO Budget

1. **Website Optimization**
   - Prioritize technical SEO improvements, such as mobile-friendliness, page speed, and navigation.
   - Cost: Minimal if done in-house; $500–$3,000 if outsourced for technical audits and fixes.

2. **Keyword Research**
   - Invest in tools like Google Keyword Planner (free), SEMrush, or Ahrefs to identify the best keywords for your business.
   - Cost: Free to $100/month.

3. **Content Creation**
   - Quality content is the backbone of SEO. Budget for blog posts, videos, or infographics that target your audience's needs.
   - Cost: $50–$300 per blog post if outsourced; DIY if in-house.

4. **Local SEO Efforts**
   - Claim and optimize your Google Business Profile, and consider local advertising opportunities.
   - Cost: Free for GBP; $50–$500 for local sponsorships or partnerships.

5. **Backlink Building**

- Focus on earning backlinks from reputable sites through partnerships, guest posting, or outreach.
- Cost: $0–$1,000 per month, depending on the approach.

6. **Analytics and Reporting**
    - Use tools like Google Analytics or paid platforms to monitor your progress and refine your strategy.
    - Cost: Free to $100/month.

7. **Training and Education**
    - Invest in online courses, webinars, or SEO certifications to improve your skills.
    - Cost: $50–$500 per course.

How to Stretch Your SEO Budget

Step 1: Prioritize Your Efforts

- Focus on the strategies that will deliver the biggest impact based on your goals.
- Example: If local traffic is your priority, invest in Google Business Profile optimization and local keyword targeting.

Step 2: Use Free and Affordable Tools

- Leverage free tools like Google Keyword Planner, Search Console, and Answer the Public for research.
- Explore affordable SEO tools like Ubersuggest for small businesses.

Step 3: Outsource Strategically

- Outsource complex tasks like technical audits or advanced content creation, but handle simpler tasks like updating meta tags in-house.

Step 4: Repurpose Existing Content

- Update old blog posts, add fresh keywords, and promote them again instead of creating new content from scratch.

Step 5: Build Partnerships

- Collaborate with local businesses or bloggers for mutual promotion and backlinks, which can reduce costs.

Real-Life Example: Maximizing a Small SEO Budget

A small pet grooming business in Austin, Texas, wanted to increase local traffic but had a limited budget. Here's how they allocated their funds:

- **$0:** Claimed and optimized their Google Business Profile.
- **$30/month:** Used Ubersuggest for keyword research.
- **$100/month:** Outsourced blog writing to create posts like "How to Keep Your Dog's Coat Healthy in Austin Summers."
- **$50:** Sponsored a local pet adoption event, earning backlinks from community organizations.

Within six months, they saw a 40% increase in website traffic and a 25% boost in bookings, all while staying under a $200/month budget.

Common Budgeting Mistakes to Avoid

1. **Spending Too Much Too Soon**

- SEO takes time. Avoid overspending on expensive tools or services in the early stages.

2. **Ignoring Free Opportunities**
    - Neglecting free resources like Google Business Profile or Search Console can waste money on unnecessary tools.

3. **Failing to Track ROI**
    - Without monitoring results, you can't determine which strategies are worth the investment.

4. **Chasing Shortcuts**
    - Avoid paying for low-quality backlinks or "guaranteed" rankings, as they can harm your SEO in the long run.

Checklist: Create Your SEO Budget Today

- Define your SEO goals and identify your top priorities.
- List the tools and services you need (e.g., keyword research, content creation).
- Research free or affordable alternatives to paid tools.
- Allocate a monthly budget for outsourced tasks, like content writing or backlink building.
- Track your results regularly to refine your spending strategy.

Budgeting for SEO doesn't have to be overwhelming. By focusing on high-impact areas and using your resources wisely, you can achieve significant results without overextending your finances. Remember, consistency and strategic planning are key to maximizing your SEO investment.

Chapter 16: Avoiding SEO Pitfalls and Mistakes

Why Avoiding SEO Mistakes Is Critical

SEO is a powerful tool, but when done incorrectly, it can waste time, money, and even harm your website's rankings. For small business owners, understanding common pitfalls can save you from setbacks and ensure your SEO efforts yield the best possible results.

In this chapter, we'll explore the most frequent mistakes businesses make with SEO and how to avoid them, empowering you to work smarter and more effectively.

Common SEO Mistakes to Avoid

1. **Ignoring Mobile Optimization**

- Over half of internet traffic comes from mobile devices, yet many businesses neglect to ensure their sites are mobile-friendly.
- **Fix It:** Use responsive web design, ensure fast page loads, and test your site on multiple devices.

2. **Keyword Stuffing**
   - Overloading your content with keywords makes it unreadable and can result in penalties from search engines.
   - **Fix It:** Focus on natural keyword placement and prioritize content quality.

3. **Neglecting Local SEO**
   - Small businesses often miss the opportunity to optimize for local searches, such as "near me" queries.
   - **Fix It:** Optimize your Google Business Profile, include location-based keywords, and encourage customer reviews.

4. **Skipping Technical SEO**
   - Broken links, slow-loading pages, and poor site structure can harm your rankings.
   - **Fix It:** Regularly audit your website using tools like Screaming Frog or SEMrush and address any technical issues.

5. **Focusing on Quantity Over Quality**
   - Publishing frequent, low-quality content won't engage your audience or rank well.

- **Fix It:** Prioritize creating fewer, high-quality pieces of content that add value to your audience.

6. **Ignoring Analytics**
    - Without tracking performance, you won't know what's working or where to improve.
    - **Fix It:** Use Google Analytics and Google Search Console to monitor key metrics like traffic, bounce rate, and conversions.

7. **Buying Links or Followers**
    - Paying for backlinks or social media followers might seem tempting, but it can lead to penalties and damage your credibility.
    - **Fix It:** Focus on earning links organically through partnerships, high-quality content, and outreach.

8. **Failing to Update Content**
    - Outdated content can lose rankings over time, especially if competitors publish more current information.
    - **Fix It:** Regularly update old blog posts and landing pages with fresh information and new keywords.

Signs Your SEO Strategy Needs Adjustments

1. **Your Rankings Are Dropping**
    - Check for new competitors, algorithm changes, or outdated strategies.
2. **Traffic Isn't Converting**

- Ensure your landing pages and CTAs align with the intent of your audience.

3. **High Bounce Rates**
   - Evaluate your website for poor design, irrelevant content, or slow loading times.

4. **Stagnant Backlink Growth**
   - A lack of new backlinks could indicate you need to promote your content more effectively.

Proactive Tips for Success

1. **Stay Updated on SEO Trends**
   - Follow industry blogs, such as Moz, Search Engine Journal, or Google's own updates, to stay informed about algorithm changes.

2. **Build Relationships for Backlinks**
   - Network with local businesses, bloggers, and influencers to earn natural backlinks.

3. **Conduct Regular SEO Audits**
   - Review your site's performance quarterly to identify issues before they escalate.

4. **Focus on User Intent**
   - Create content that answers specific questions or solves problems for your target audience.

5. **Be Patient**
   - SEO takes time to show results. Avoid drastic changes based on short-term fluctuations.

Real-Life Example: Recovering from an SEO Mistake

A small home cleaning service in Miami made the mistake of over-optimizing their site with too many keywords, including irrelevant ones. Their pages became unreadable, and their rankings dropped.

After seeking help, they focused on creating user-friendly content with natural keyword placement, optimized their Google Business Profile, and built relationships with local bloggers for backlinks. Within six months, their rankings improved, and website traffic increased by 35%.

Checklist: Avoid SEO Mistakes Today

- Ensure your website is mobile-friendly and loads quickly.
- Review your content for natural keyword usage and quality.
- Perform a technical SEO audit to fix broken links and improve site structure.
- Monitor your analytics and adjust your strategy based on performance.
- Update old content with fresh information and keywords.

Closing Thoughts on SEO Pitfalls

Mistakes are a natural part of any learning process, but by staying proactive and informed, you can minimize their impact and keep your SEO strategy on track. With the right approach, even setbacks can become opportunities for growth and improvement.

Chapter 17: Staying Motivated and Consistent

Why Consistency Is Key in SEO

SEO is a long-term strategy, not a one-time effort. The algorithms and competition are constantly evolving, and staying ahead requires ongoing attention and adaptation. While the journey to improved rankings and increased traffic may take time, consistency is the factor that transforms small, steady efforts into significant results.

For small business owners, the challenge isn't just about knowing what to do—it's about maintaining the motivation to keep going when progress feels slow. This final chapter will equip you with the mindset and strategies needed to stay committed to your SEO goals.

The Benefits of Patience and Persistence

1. **Compounding Results**
   - SEO efforts build on each other. Every optimized page, new backlink, or piece of content you create strengthens your overall performance.

2. **Increased Authority**
   - Over time, consistent updates and quality content establish your business as a trusted authority in your niche.

3. **Sustainable Growth**
   - Unlike paid advertising, which stops when the budget runs out, SEO delivers long-term value that grows with your business.

Strategies for Staying Motivated

Step 1: Set Realistic Expectations

- Understand that SEO is a marathon, not a sprint. Results often take months to materialize, so celebrate small wins along the way.

Step 2: Break Down Goals

- Divide your SEO plan into manageable tasks.
    - Example: Focus on optimizing one page, writing one blog, or earning one backlink each week.

Step 3: Track Your Progress

- Use tools like Google Analytics to monitor improvements in traffic, rankings, and engagement.
- Celebrate milestones, such as increased conversions or hitting a new ranking for a target keyword.

Step 4: Stay Educated

- Follow industry updates through blogs, webinars, or newsletters. Staying informed keeps you inspired and adaptable.

Step 5: Build a Routine

- Dedicate a consistent time each week for SEO tasks. Treat it as an essential part of your business operations.

Step 6: Seek Support

- Join online communities or local business groups where you can share challenges, tips, and successes with other entrepreneurs.

Tools to Keep You on Track

1. **SEO Task Management**
    - Use tools like Trello, Asana, or Monday.com to organize and track your SEO to-do list.
2. **Analytics and Reporting**
    - Set up automated reports in Google Analytics or SEMrush to track progress without constant manual checks.
3. **Content Scheduling**
    - Use platforms like Buffer, Hootsuite, or HubSpot to plan and automate content distribution.

Real-Life Example: The Power of Consistency

A small bike repair shop in Denver started their SEO journey with minimal knowledge but a commitment to consistent efforts. Every week, they:

- Published one blog post optimized for local keywords, such as "How to Winterize Your Bike in Denver."
- Requested backlinks from local cycling blogs.
- Updated their Google Business Profile with customer reviews and seasonal promotions.

Over 12 months, their website traffic tripled, and they became the top-ranking shop for "bike repair in Denver." The key? Small, steady steps and a willingness to learn as they went.

Common Reasons Businesses Lose Motivation

1. **Impatience**

- Expecting overnight results can lead to frustration.

2. **Lack of Clear Goals**
    - Without specific milestones, progress can feel aimless.

3. **Overwhelm**
    - Trying to tackle too much at once can lead to burnout.

4. **Neglecting the Basics**
    - Ignoring foundational SEO practices can make advanced efforts less effective.

Checklist: Build Long-Term SEO Habits Today

- Set a realistic timeline for your SEO goals (e.g., 6 months to rank for local keywords).
- Dedicate at least one hour a week to SEO tasks.
- Celebrate small wins, like improved rankings or increased website traffic.
- Join an SEO community or business group for support.
- Commit to ongoing learning through blogs, webinars, or online courses.

Final Thoughts

SEO is not about perfection—it's about persistence. Small, consistent efforts over time will yield meaningful results for your business. By staying motivated and committed, you're not just optimizing for search engines; you're building a stronger, more resilient foundation for your business's success.

As you move forward, remember that every action you take, no matter how small, contributes to your long-term growth. The journey may have its challenges, but the rewards are worth it.

www.ingramcontent.com/pod-product-compliance
Lightning Source LLC
Chambersburg PA
CBHW050325230526
45471CB00005B/2358